Alfred's

Music for Little Mozarts

Written Activities and Playing Examples to Reinforce Note-Reading

The *Notespeller & Sight-Play Book 3* reinforces note-reading skills based on the concepts introduced in the *Music Lesson Book 3*. The pages in this book correlate page by page with the materials in the *Music Lesson Book*. They should be assigned according to the instructions in the upper right corner of the pages in this book. They also may be assigned as review material at any time after the students have passed the designated *Music Lesson Book* page.

Each page of the *Notespeller & Sight-Play Book* has two activities—a written activity and a playing example. The written activity reinforces notes on the keyboard and the staff through coloring, circling, drawing, or matching. The sight-play examples help students:

• Relate notes and musical concepts to performance on the keyboard.

• Move out of fixed hand positions.

• Identify melodic and rhythm patterns.

For the sight-play examples, teachers may use the following preparation steps:

1 Clap (or tap) the rhythm and count aloud evenly.

2 Point to the notes and rests and count aloud evenly.

3 Play and say the finger numbers.

4 Point to the notes and say the note names.

5 Play and say the note names.

Alfred Music
P.O. Box 10003
Van Nuys, CA 91410-0003

Illustrations by Christine Finn

D1275267

Christine H. Barden · Gayle Kowalchyk · E. L. Lancaster

ISBN-10: 1-4706-3241-1
ISBN-13: 978-1-4706-3241-0

Use with Alfred's Music for Little Mozarts, Lesson Book 3, page 5.

Steps and Skips in Middle C Position

Draw a line connecting the dots to match the notes to their letter names.

skip down

step up

skip up

step down

E–F

G–E

G–F

A–C

Sight-Play

Play and count.

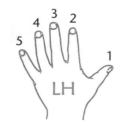
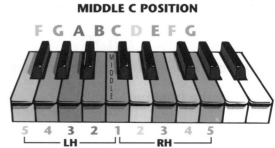
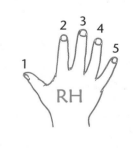

MIDDLE C POSITION

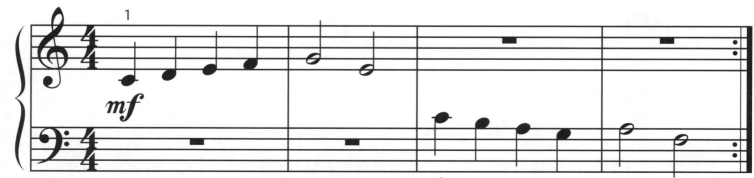

Count: 1   1   1   1   1 – 2   1 – 2

More Steps and Skips in Middle C Position

Draw a line connecting the dots to match the notes to their letter names.

Sight-Play

MIDDLE C POSITION

Play and count.

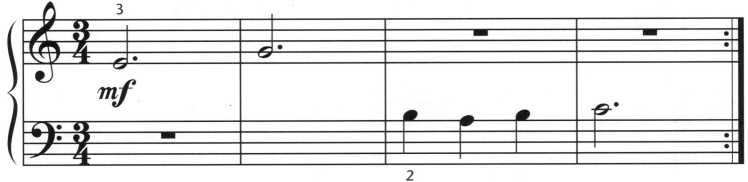

Count: 1   –   2   –   3   1   1   1   1

Use with page 8.

C in Bass Clef

The music friends just found space note Bass C.
Trace the Bass C whole notes.

Sight-Play

The music friends want you to try this funny trick.
Use different LH fingers to play space note Bass C.

Play and count.

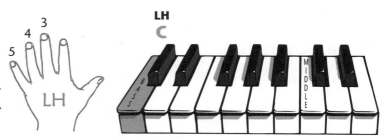

Count: 1 – 2   rest – 2

D in Bass Clef

The music friends just found line note D.
Trace the D whole notes.

Sight-Play

The music friends want you to try this funny trick.
Use different LH fingers to play line note D.

Play and count.

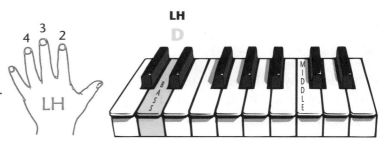

mf

Count: 1   –   2   rest   –   2

Use with page 11.

E in Bass Clef

Professor Haydn Hippo just found space note E.
Trace the E whole notes.

Sight-Play

Professor Haydn Hippo wants you to try this funny trick. Use different LH fingers to play space note E.

Play and count.

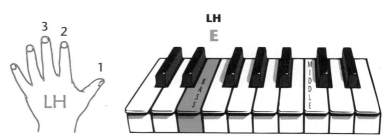

f

Count: 1   –   2   rest

C, D, and E in Bass Clef

Help the music friends name the notes.
Draw a line connecting the dots to match each note to its letter name.

Sight-Play

Play and count.

mf

Count: 1 – 2   1 – 2   1   1   1 – 2

C Position in Bass Clef

Help Mozart Mouse name the notes.
Draw a line connecting the dots to match each note to its letter name.

Use with page 14.

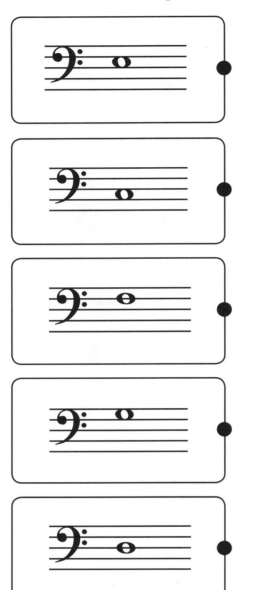

G

F

E

D

C

Sight-Play

Play and count.

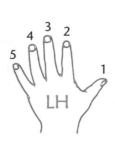

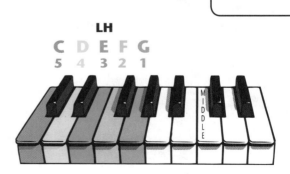

Count: 1 – 2   1   1 – 2 – 3

C Position on the Grand Staff

Help the music friends find the notes in C Position
on the Grand Staff.

1 Circle each C with a **green** crayon.

2 Circle each D with a **yellow** crayon.

3 Circle each E with a **red** crayon.

4 Circle each F with a **pink** crayon.

5 Circle each G with an **orange** crayon.

Sight-Play

Play and count.

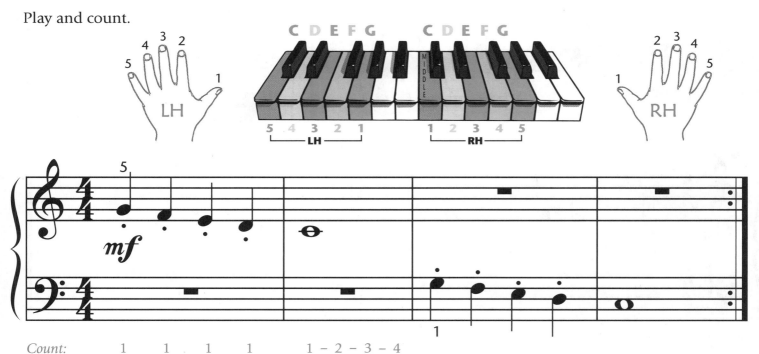

Count: 1   1   1   1   1 – 2 – 3 – 4

Use with page 17.

Steps in Middle C Position

Draw a line connecting the dots to match the notes to their letter names.

step down

A–G

step up

B–C

step down

D–E

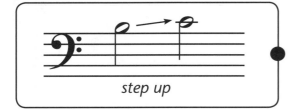
step up

G–F

Sight-Play

Play and count.

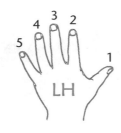
LH

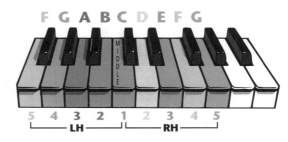

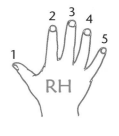
RH

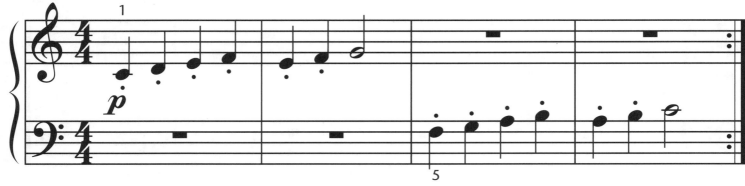

Count: 1 1 1 1   1 1 1 – 2

Skips in Middle C Position

Draw a line connecting the dots to match
the notes to their letter names.

E–G

B–G

F–A

F–D

Sight-Play

Play and count.

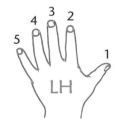

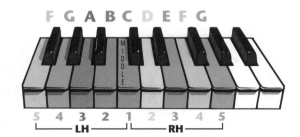

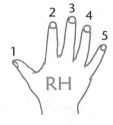

Count: 1   1   1   1 – 2 – 3

2nds in Treble Clef

Nina Ballerina discovered that steps and 2nds are the same.

Draw a line connecting the dots to match the 2nds in treble clef to their letter names.

up a 2nd

F–E

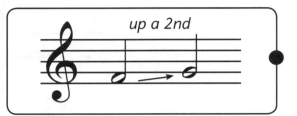

down a 2nd

D–C

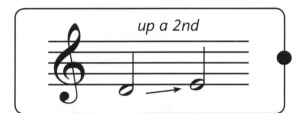

up a 2nd

F–G

down a 2nd

D–E

Sight-Play

RH C POSITION

Play and count.

mf

Count: 1 – 2   1   1 – 2 – 3

2nds in Bass Clef

Draw a line connecting the dots to match the 2nds in bass clef to their letter names.

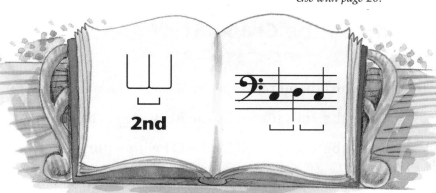

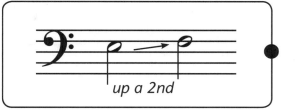
up a 2nd

F–E

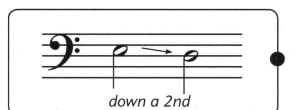
down a 2nd

E–F

up a 2nd

F–G

down a 2nd

E–D

Sight-Play

LH C POSITION

Play and count.

Use with page 21.

2nds on the Grand Staff

Decide which hand plays the 2nds on the Grand Staff.

1 Circle the 2nds played by the RH with a **red** crayon.

2 Circle the 2nds played by the LH with a **purple** crayon.

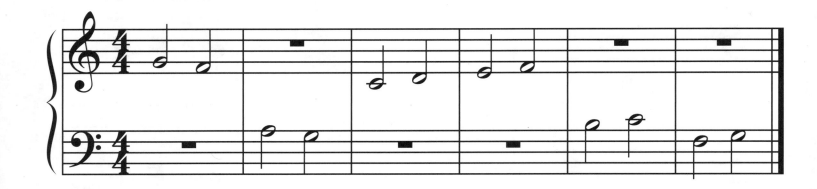

Sight-Play

MIDDLE C POSITION

Play and count.

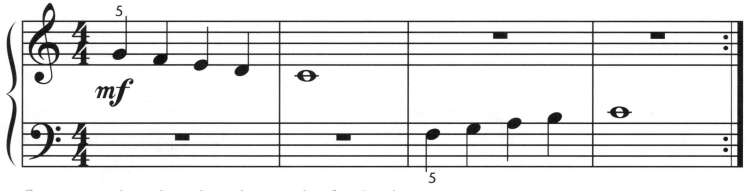

Count: 1   1   1   1   1 – 2 – 3 – 4

3rds in Treble Clef

Draw a line connecting the dots to match the 3rds in treble clef to their letter names.

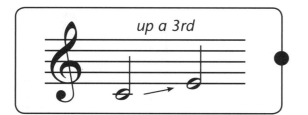

up a 3rd

E–C

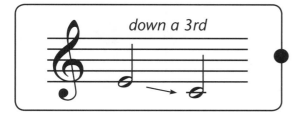

down a 3rd

F–D

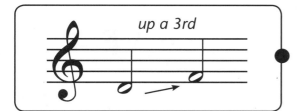

up a 3rd

C–E

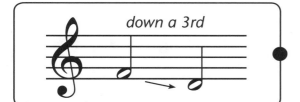

down a 3rd

D–F

Sight-Play

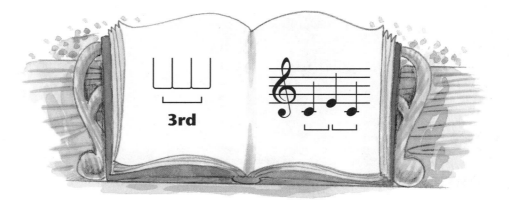

RH C POSITION

Play and count.

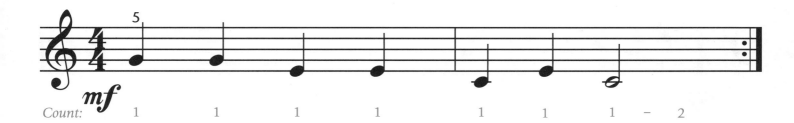

Count: 1   1   1   1   1   1   1 – 2

Use with page 23.

3rds in Bass Clef

Draw a line connecting the dots to match the 3rds in bass clef to their letter names.

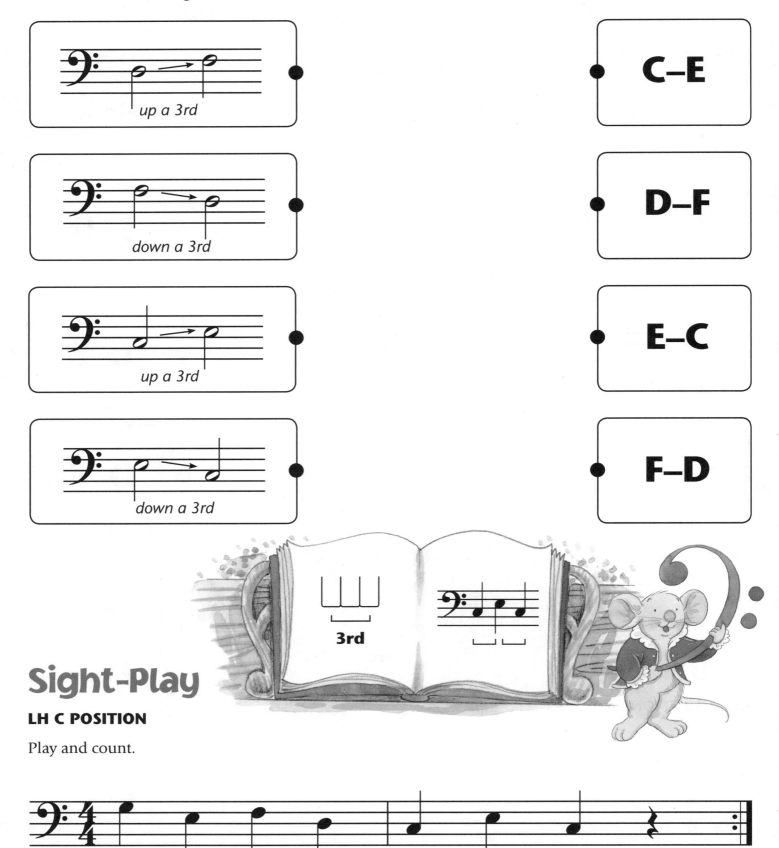

up a 3rd

down a 3rd

up a 3rd

down a 3rd

C–E

D–F

E–C

F–D

3rd

Sight-Play

LH C POSITION

Play and count.

mf

Count: 1   1   1   1   1   1   1   rest

More 3rds in Bass Clef

Draw a line connecting the dots to match the 3rds in bass clef to their letter names.

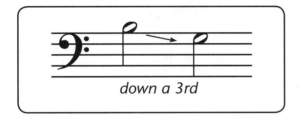
up a 3rd

A–C

down a 3rd

G–B

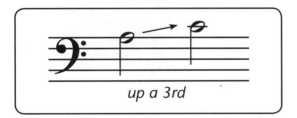
up a 3rd

C–A

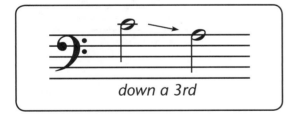
down a 3rd

B–G

Sight-Play

LH MIDDLE C POSITION

Play and count.

Count: **mf** ⁴ 1 – 2 1   1 – 2 – 3

Use with page 27.

2nds and 3rds in Middle C Position

Help Beethoven Bear circle the intervals.

1 Circle each 2nd with a **green** crayon.

2 Circle each 3rd with a **red** crayon.

Sight-Play

MIDDLE C POSITION

Play and count.

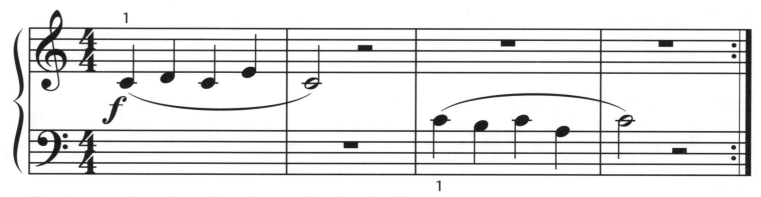

Count: 1   1   1   1   1 – 2 rest – 2

2nds and 3rds in C Position

Help the music friends circle the intervals.

1 Circle each 2nd with a **blue** crayon.

2 Circle each 3rd with an **orange** crayon.

Sight-Play

C POSITION

Play and count.

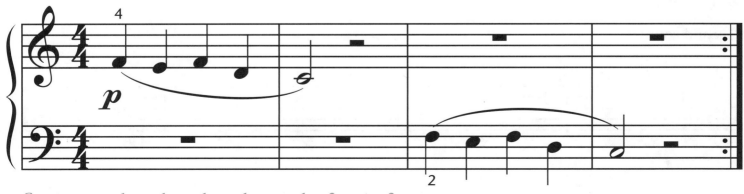

Count: 1   1   1   1   1 – 2 rest – 2

Melodic and Harmonic Intervals in Treble Clef

Help Pachelbel Penguin circle the melodic and harmonic intervals in treble clef.

1 Circle each melodic interval with a **purple** crayon.

2 Circle each harmonic interval with a **blue** crayon.

Sight-Play

RH C POSITION

Play and count.

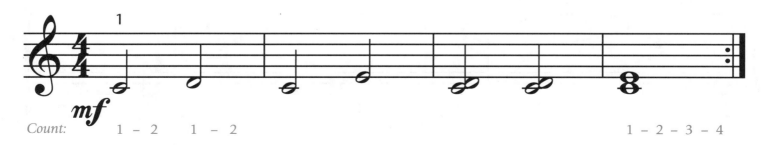

Count: 1 – 2   1 – 2   1 – 2 – 3 – 4

Melodic and Harmonic Intervals in Bass Clef

Help the music friends circle the melodic and harmonic intervals in bass clef.

1 Circle each melodic interval with a **red** crayon.

2 Circle each harmonic interval with a **green** crayon.

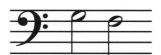

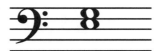

Sight-Play

LH C POSITION

Play and count.

Count: **f** ¹   1 – 2   1 – 2   1 – 2 – 3 – 4

Use with page 32.

More About Melodic and Harmonic Intervals

Draw a line connecting the dots to match the melodic and harmonic intervals to their letter names.

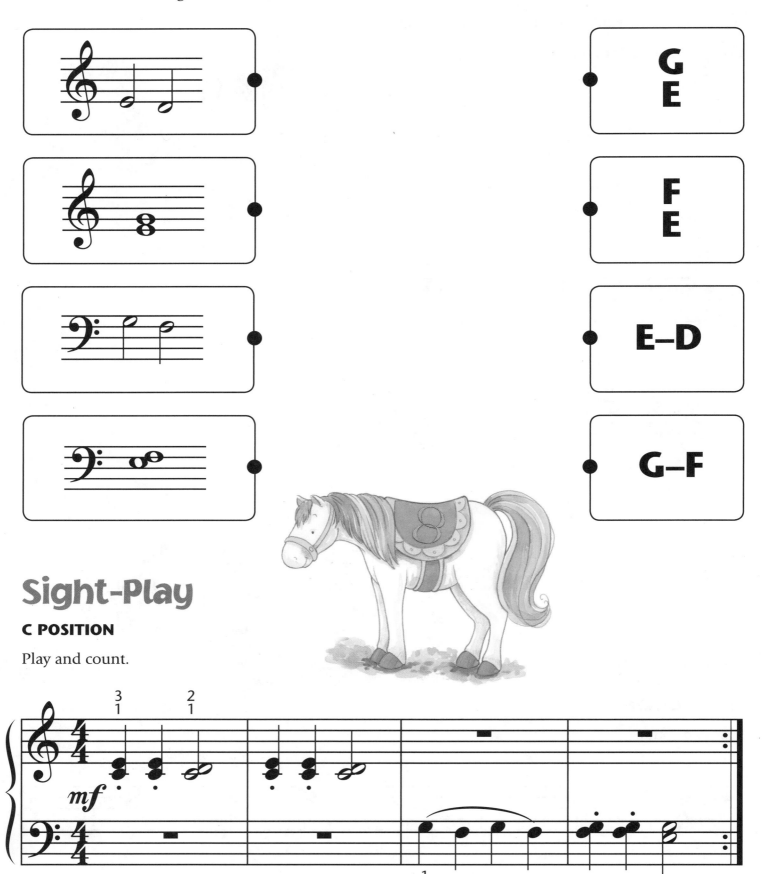

Sight-Play

C POSITION

Play and count.

Count: 1   1   1 – 2

Hands Together in C Position

Help Clara Schumann-Cat name notes that are played hands together.
Circle the correct note names.

G or **G**
D   **F**

(circle one)

D or **E**
C   **C**

(circle one)

G or **F**
F   **G**

(circle one)

Sight-Play

C POSITION

Play and count.

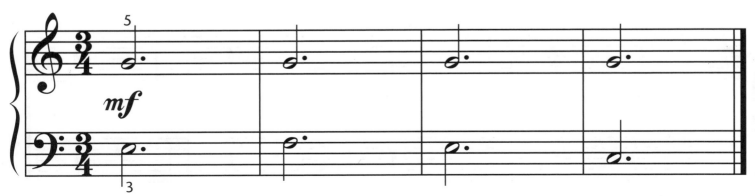

Count: 1 – 2 – 3

Use with page 37.

Hands Together in Middle C Position

Help Professor Haydn Hippo name notes that are played hands together.
Circle the correct note names.

G		**G**
G	or	**B**

(circle one)

F		**D**
C	or	**C**

(circle one)

A		**E**
E	or	**A**

(circle one)

Sight-Play

MIDDLE C POSITION

Play and count.

Count: 1 – 2 – 3   rest

4ths in Middle C Position

Draw a line connecting the dots to match the 4ths in Middle C Position to their letter names.

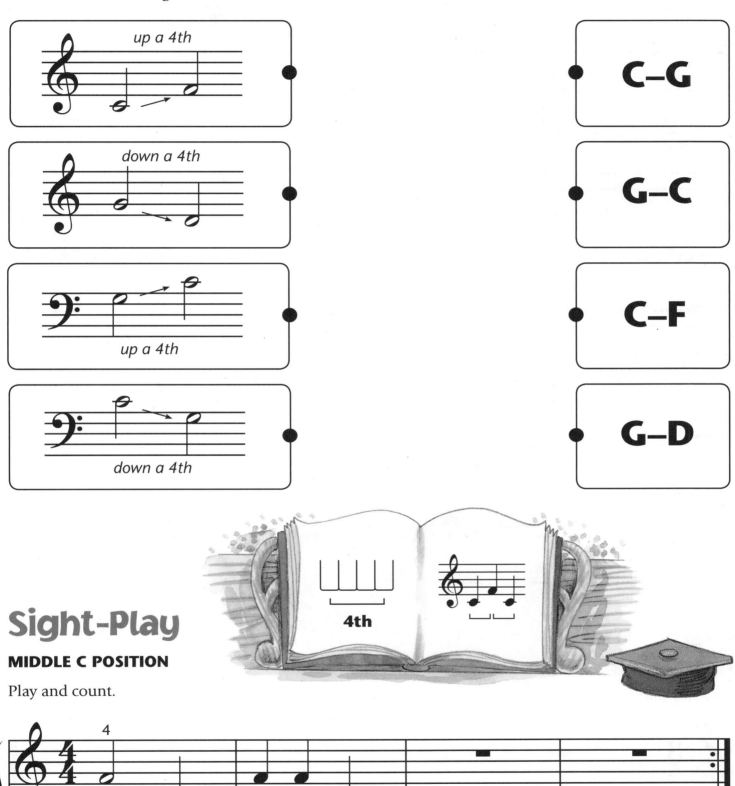

Sight-Play

MIDDLE C POSITION

Play and count.

Count: 1 – 2   1 – 2   1   1   1 – 2

4ths in C Position

Use with page 39.

Draw a line connecting the dots to match
the 4ths in C Position to their letter names.

D–G

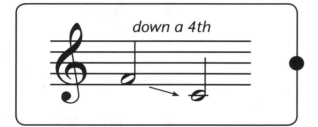

C–F

G–D

F–C

Sight-Play

C POSITION

Play and count.

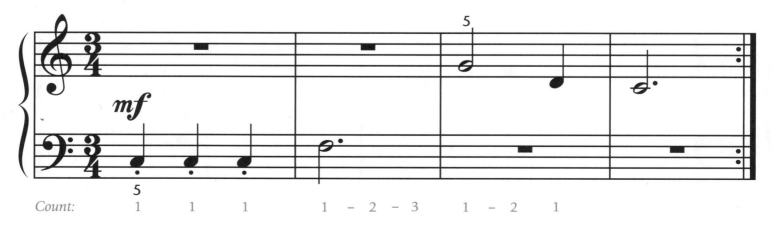

Count: 1   1   1   1 – 2 – 3   1 – 2   1

4ths on the Grand Staff

Decide which hand plays the 4ths on the Grand Staff.

1 Circle each 4th played by the RH with a **red** crayon.

2 Circle each 4th played by the LH with a **purple** crayon.

Sight-Play

MIDDLE C POSITION

Play and count.

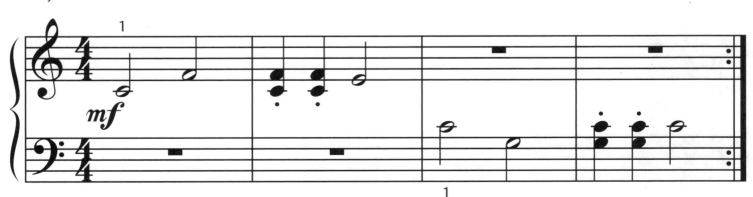

Count: 1 – 2   1 – 2   1   1   1 – 2

Use with page 42.

5ths in C Position

Draw a line connecting the dots to match the 5ths in C Position to their letter names.

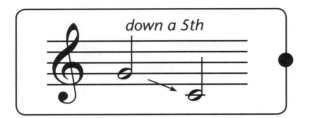

G–C

C–G

Sight-Play

C POSITION

Play and count.

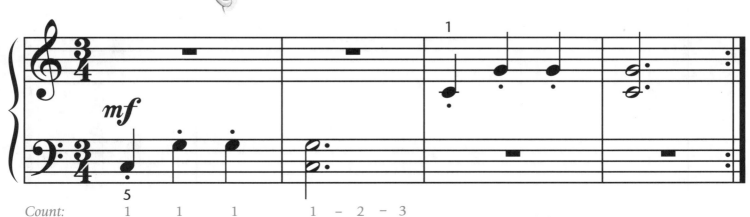

Count: 1   1   1   1 – 2 – 3

5ths in Middle C Position

Draw a line connecting the dots to match the
5ths in Middle C Position to their letter names.

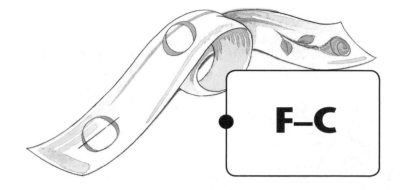

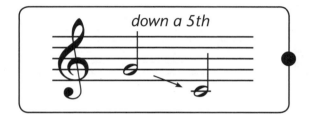

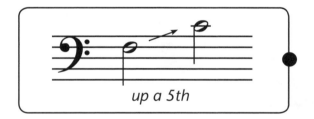

Sight-Play

MIDDLE C POSITION

Play and count.

Use with page 44.

Melodic and Harmonic 5ths

1 Circle each melodic 5th with a **red** crayon.

2 Circle each harmonic 5th with a **purple** crayon.

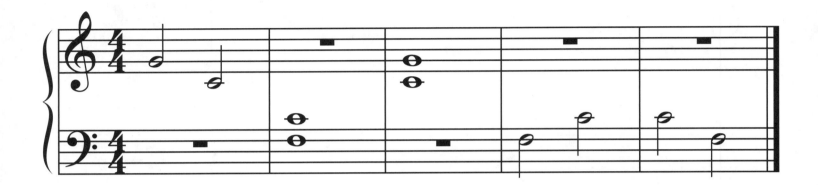

Sight-Play

C POSITION

Play and count.

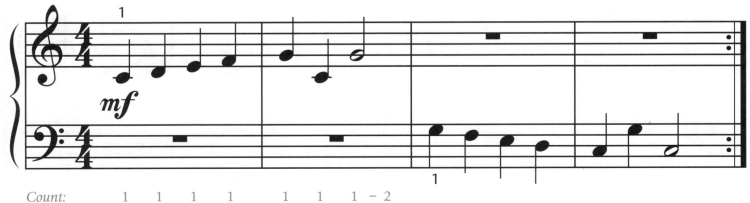

Count: 1 1 1 1   1 1 1 – 2

Review: 2nds and 3rds

① Circle each 2nd with a **red** crayon.

② Circle each 3rd with a **purple** crayon.

Sight-Play

MIDDLE C POSITION

Play and count.

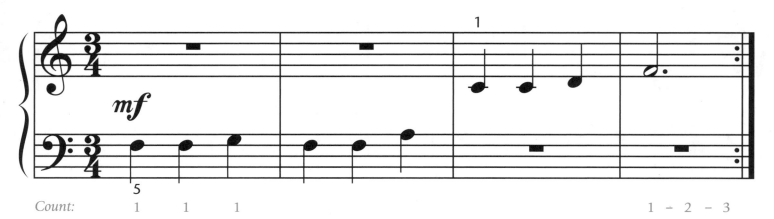

Count: 1   1   1   1 – 2 – 3

Use with page 47.

Review: 4ths and 5ths

1 Circle each 4th with a **red** crayon.

2 Circle each 5th with a **purple** crayon.

Sight-Play

C POSITION

Play and count.

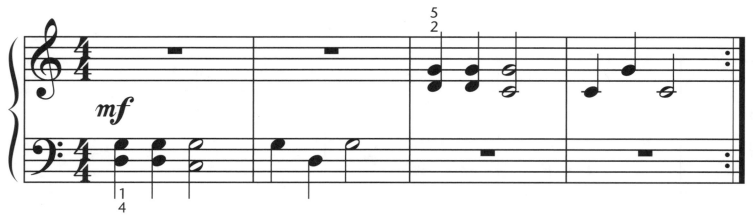

Count: 1   1   1 – 2